ANCIENT INDIAN WISDOM

ANCIENT INDIAN WISDOM

Spiritual Insights for Modern Life

MICHAEL KERRIGAN

amber
BOOKS

MIX
Paper | Supporting responsible forestry
FSC® C017606
www.fsc.org

Amber Books Ltd
United House
North Road
London N7 9DP
United Kingdom
www.amberbooks.co.uk
Facebook: amberbooks
YouTube: amberbooksltd
Instagram: amberbooksltd
X(Twitter): @amberbooks

ISBN: 978-1-83886-720-1

Design & Editorial: Amber Books Ltd

Printed in China

TRADITIONAL CHINESE BOOKBINDING

This book has been produced using traditional Chinese bookbinding techniques, using a method that was developed during the Ming Dynasty (1368–1644) and remained in use until the adoption of Western binding techniques in the early 1900s. In traditional Chinese binding, single sheets of paper are printed on one side only, and each sheet is folded in half, with the printed pages on the outside. The book block is then sandwiched between two boards and sewn together through punched holes close to the cut edges of the folded sheets.

Contents

Introduction

India, said the Swami Vivekananda, one of modern Hinduism's most important thinkers, 'is the ancient land where wisdom made its home'. Some of the sayings and quotations here are indeed of immense antiquity but they still seem fresh and timely to this day. For, 3,000 years and more ago, the first Indian poets and thinkers were drawn to those deep universals of existence which have applied in every age since then and struck a chord in every single culture.

Down the centuries, of course, India has constantly renewed its thinking. Several great religions – not just Hinduism but Jainism, Buddhism, Sikhism – started here. Sometimes the ideas flowing from these faiths have been abstruse or even mystical: in their essentials, though, they have always been quite simple. 'Non-injury is the highest duty,' one ancient shloka or saying has it, setting down a cornerstone of Indian belief. 'Earth is my mother,' says the Atharvaveda (c. 1000 BCE), establishing the first principles of a way of thinking that was eco-conscious from the very start.

Ultimately, though, the highest objective of Indian wisdom – as of any other nation's – is the clearest possible understanding of our lives. Not just in the big existential picture but in the more down-to-earth and practical issues we find ourselves facing day-to-day. Here, then, are thoughts on home life and family relations as well as on the joys and travails of romantic passion and the moral duties we owe to those around us. Here too are insights into the influences that shape us as individuals and the higher understandings we may need to be truly 'wise'.

Integrity is key and, not for the first or last time, Chanakya said it best. Famous as adviser to the Mauryan Emperor Chandragupta in around the fourth century BCE, he has been an inspiration to Indians ever since. 'Nothing is unattainable to the truthful,' he concluded.

सर्वतीर्थमयी माता सर्वदेवमयः पिता ।
मातरं पितरं चैव यस्तु कुर्यात्प्रदक्षिणम् ॥ १९॥

'A mother is the embodiment of all pilgrimage places;
a father the embodiment of all the gods.'

– Padma purana, fourth–fifteenth century CE

गुरूणां माता गरीयसी ।।

'A mother is the greatest teacher.'

– Chanakya, c. fourth century BCE

सन्तुष्टो भार्यया भर्ता भर्त्रा भार्या तथैव च ।
यस्मिन्नेव कुले नित्यं कल्याणं तत्र वै
ध्रुवम् ॥ ६० ॥

'In that family in which the husband is pleased with the wife and the wife with the husband, happiness will assuredly be lasting.'

– Manusmriti, c. second century CE

न पुत्रसंस्पर्शात् परं सुखम् ।।

'No pleasure is greater than the touch of one's children.'

– Chanakya, c. fourth century BCE

श्रवश्यं पितुराचारः॥

‘A father’s rule is binding on a son.’

– *Traditional saying*

कुलानुरूपं वृत्तम् ॥

'Conduct should befit family.'

– Chanakya, c. fourth century BCE

अमनद्धयं ज्ञातदि्वं ाक्यं ॥

'An evil world from a cousin is insufferable.'

– Indian proverb

न ग्रहं एरहमत्ियाङ्गरे दणी एहम् च्यते ॥

'It is not the house but the housewife that makes the home.'

– Indian proverb

वित्तेन रक्ष्यते धर्मो विद्या योगेन रक्ष्यते ।
मृदुना रक्ष्यते भूपः सत्स्त्रिया रक्ष्यते गृहम् ॥

'Righteousness is protected by wealth, learning by practice, the ruler by gentleness, the home by a good woman.'

– Chanakya, c. fourth century BCE

नारीणां ग्दषणएं पतः ॥

'A husband is the ornament of women.'

– Ancient saying

यदि किंचिद् दोषः किं धनेन कुलेन किं ॥

'If there be defect in the son-in-law,
what is wealth and what is birth?'

– Indian proverb

यादृशौ माता तादृशी पुची॥

'Like mother, like daughter.'

– Indian proverb

प्रर गरदं परमस्खं चरिाचाच्छनकसमानः॥

‘In the father-in-law’s house the greatest happiness
is found at first, but after the third night
the son-in-law is treated like a dog.’

– *Anonymous*

सत्पुचः कुलदीपकः ॥

'A good son is the light of his family.'

– *Ancient saying*

यस्यास्तु न भवेद् भ्राता न विज्ञायेत वा पिता ।
नोपयच्छेत तां प्राज्ञः पुत्रिकाधर्मशङ्कया ॥
११॥

'The wise man will not marry a woman who has no brother – or whose father is unknown – for fear of her having the character of the "appointed daughter".'

– Manusmriti, c. second century CE

यत्र नार्यस्तु पूज्यन्ते रमन्ते तत्र देवताः ।
यत्रैतास्तु न पूज्यन्ते सर्वास्तत्राफलाः क्रियाः
॥ ५६॥

'Where women are honoured, there the gods rejoice.
Where they are not honoured, there all other rites
and offerings are fruitless.'

– Manusmriti, c. second century CE

मातृदेवो भव । पितृदेवो भव ।

'Be one to whom a mother is as a god;
be one to whom a father is as a god.'

– *Taittiriya upanishad, c. sixth century BCE*

देवीरापः शुद्धा वोडदवः सुपरिविष्टा देवेषु
सुपरिविष्टा वयं परिवेष्टारो भूयास्म ॥१३॥

'Women, pure and cool as celestial waters, marry by choice
and settle with noble men in security and protection.
So should we men, settled and secure with the women,
be their guardians and protectors, in love and duty.'

– *Yajurveda, c. 1000 BCE*

बालादप्यर्थजातं शृणुयात् ।।

'Meaningful words, even from a child, should be listened to.'

– Chanakya, c. fourth century BCE

सुखस्य मुलं धर्मः

'Righteousness is the root of happiness.'

– Chanakya, c. fourth century BCE

खहि सा परमो धर्मः॥

'Non-injury is the highest duty.'

– Traditional Sanskrit saying

कोपः पापस्य कारणं ॥

'Anger is a cause of sin.'

– Traditional saying

अर्था गृहे निवर्तन्ते श्मशाने मित्रबान्धवाः।
सुकृतं दुष्कृतं चैव गच्छन्तमनुगच्छति॥

'Wealth stops at the house; friends and relations at the grave; good and evil actions follow the dying man.'

– *Anonymous*

एकः पापानि कुरुते फलं भुङ्क्ते महाजनः ॥

'One sins, many suffer.'

– Indian proverb

यदि ददयमप्टद् तस्य सर्व वरिुद्धं ॥

'If the heart is impure, all its actions will be wrong.'

– Indian proverb

यः परार्थुपसर्पति स सत्पुरूषः ॥

'He is a good man who moves forward to help others.'

– Chanakya, c. fourth century BCE

वुश्धकिस्य वषिं पुच्छं मच्तकाया वषिं भरिः।
भृजंगस्य वषिं द्रा सर्वांगं दुर्जने वषिं ॥

‘A scorpion’s venom is in his tail, a fly’s
in his head, a serpent’s in his fang … but a bad man’s
poison permeates his whole body.’

– Anonymous

षाक्नाद्धर्पिंकस्य दूरादस्पर्शनं वरं ॥

'Steering clear of the mud is better than washing it off afterwards.'

– Indian proverb

नास्त्यलस्यैहिकामुष्मिकम् ।।

'The lazy cannot hope for success either in this world or the other.'

– *Chanakya, c. fourth century BCE*

अव्यवस्थतिवन्तिस्य प्रसादोपि भयंकरः ॥

'Even the favour of an ill-regulated man is to be dreaded.'

– *Anonymous*

श्रल्पविद्यो महागर्वः

‘Little learning, much pride.’

– *Indian proverb*

नमंति फलनिो चा नमंति गुणनिो जनाः ॥

'Fruitful trees bend; men of wisdom stoop humbly.'

– Indian proverb

नास्ति खलस्य मित्रम्

'The wicked have no friends.'

– Chanakya, c. fourth century BCE

एकसारथप्रयात ये नःस्वमरथार्धनि नरम्॥५६॥
अपास्य स्वानन्नतर्ता ते इमे श्लेष्पभोजनिः।

‘Those who eat their own food, ignoring their companion who is destitute and in need of help, are destined to find that they are feeding on phlegm.’

– Markandeya purana, c. 250 CE

नास्त्यप्राप्यं सत्यवताम् ॥

‘Nothing is unattainable by the truthful.’

– Chanakya, c. fourth century BCE

साता चरूख्रि खो द्धं सत्रुथ्च्रियाः।
गरियस्ते पर्वता हमिवन्तोऽरण्यं ते पृथवि
स्योनमस्तु।

'Oh Earth, may your hills, your snow-capped mountains, your forests be comfortable for us.'

– *Atharvaveda, c. 1000 BCE*

आत्मवत्सर्वश्चतानि यः पश्यति सउ पश्यति ॥

'He who looks on all living things as himself, truly sees.'

– Anonymous

यथोर्णनाभिः सृजते गृह्णते च यथा
पृथिव्यामोषधयः सम्भवन्ति ।
यथा सतः पुरुषात् केशलोमानि तथाक्षरात्
सम्भवतीह विश्वम् ॥

'As the spider casts out and draws in its web, as on the earth the annual herbs are produced, as from living man the hairs of the head and body spring forth, so is produced the universe from the indestructible Brahman.'

– Mundaka Upanishad, c. fifth century BCE

दूरस्थाः पर्वता रम्यास्ममीपम्धास्तु बर्बराः ॥

'Mountains are beautiful at a distance, rugged when near.'

– *Traditional*

यस्तु सर्वाणि भूतान्यात्मन्येवानुपश्यति
सर्वभूतेषु चात्मानं ततो न विजुगुप्सते ॥

'Whoever beholds all beings in the soul alone, and the soul in all beings, does hence not look down on any creation.'

– Isa Upanishad, c. 500 BCE

आ यातु मित्र ऋतुभिः कल्पमानः संवेशयन्
पृथिवीमुस्रियाभिः ।
अथास्मभ्यं वरुणो वायुरग्निर्बृहद् राष्ट्रं
संवेश्यं दधातु ॥

'Let the sun come equipped with seasons, lulling the earth to rest with gleams of splendour. And so let rainy water, air and fire make our dominion tranquil and exalted.'

– Atharvaveda, c. 1000 BCE

सवषि्रमैः सस्मतिजह्यिवीषतिैर् वलिासवत्या
मनर्सा प्रवासनिाम्।
अनङ्गसन्दीपनम् आशु कुर्वता यथा प्रदोषाः
शशचिारूभूषणाः॥ १-९२

'Spring sees the lovely young women smile,
their sidelong glances mysterious as moonlit twilights,
so adorned they wake the Love God
slumbering in every passer-by.'

– Kalidasa, ritusamhara ('medley of the seasons'), fifth century CE

काशांशुका विकचपद्ममनोज्ञवक्त्रा
सोन्मादहंसरवनूपुरनादरम्या।
आपक्वशालिरुचिरा तनुगात्रयष्टिः
प्राप्ता शरन्नववधूरिव रूपरम्या॥ ३-१

'The rains have gone and Autumn come, in beauty like a bride;
flushed in the face like loving lotuses, her gown as white
as the flowered field grass or the amorous swans she passes.
Ripe rice-stalks nod in her hair as she walks …'

– Kalidasa, ritusamhara ('medley of the seasons'), fifth century CE

तारागणप्रवरभूषणम् उद्वहन्ती
मेघावरोधपरिमुक्तशशाङ्कवक्ता।
ज्योत्स्नादुकूलम् अमलम् रजनी दधाना
वृद्धिम् प्रयात्य् अनुदिनम् प्रमदेव बाला॥ ३-७

'As day by day a girl ripens to maidenly maturity
so the autumnal nights grow longer successively.'

– Kalidasa, ritusamhara ('medley of the seasons'), fifth century CE

उतेयं भूमिर्वरुणस्य राज्ञो उतद्यौ र्बृहती
ऋतसादना ।उतो द्धयः कुक्षयः कुक्षयं
उत,एतस्मन्निनल्प उदके नलीनः ॥

This earth, as well as that high heaven at a vast distance,
is God's possession. Both the oceans are God's loins;
and this small drop of water, too, contains him.

– Atharvaveda, c. 1000 BCE

निर्वनो वध्यते व्याघ्रो निर्व्याघ्रं छिद्यते वनम् ।
तस्माद्व्याघ्रो वनं रक्षेद्वनं व्याघ्रं च पालयेत् ॥

'The tiger dies without the forest, and the forest is cut down without the tiger. The tiger should defend the forest, and the forest protect the tiger.'

– *Mahabharata, c. 400 BCE*

ओं ईशावास्यमिदं सर्वं यत् किञ्च जगत्यां जगत्।
तेन त्यक्तेन भुञ्जीथा मा गृधः कस्य
स्विद्धनम्॥ १॥

'All that moves in this earth of ours is dwelt in by the Lord. Enjoy what he has allotted you, and do not covet more, by way of further wealth.'

– Isha Upanishad, c. 500 BCE

तम आसीत्तमसा ग ूढमग्रे ऽप्रके तं
सलिलं सर्वा इदम् ।तुच्छ्ये नाभ्वपहितिं
यदासीत्तपसस्तन्महिनाजायतैकम् ॥

'What was to come to be at first lay lost
in utter emptiness
but eventually warmth was born
and things started to take form.
Desire – kama – was the impulse that first stirred
creation into being
The starting seed from which
our consciousness would spring.'

– *Rig Veda, c. 1500 BCE*

कं न वशीकुरुते भुवि रामा॥

'Whom on earth will a handsome woman not subdue?'

– Bhartrari, fifth century CE

ओदुंबराणां पुष्पाणां श्च्वैतवणच्च वायसं ।
मव्यपादं जले पश्ये ननारी द द् यस्थतिं ॥

'The flowers of the fig tree, a white-coloured crow,
a fish's foot in the water … we may see all these,
but not what is going on in a woman's mind.'

– *Anonymous*

स्तीरननं दुष्कुलादपा ॥

'Take an excellent woman, even from a low caste.'

– *Ancient saying*

नीचैरवास्यन्त्युपरि च मया पान्थसङ्गात् स्मरेथा-
स्तस्याः सद्यः प्रतनिवपदं पश्यतो लब्धमेकम् ।
तन्वौ तन्वन् परिलघु हृदयं सद्यो वासोविमिश्रं
कान्तोदन्तः कथमनुगतः स्वागताङ्गेषु मनुजः ॥

'True love, no time nor distance can destroy,
And independent of all present joy,
It grows in absence, as renewed delight,
Some dear memorial, some loved lines excite.'

– Kalidasa, meghaduta ('cloud messenger'), c. fifth century CE

निपातयन्त्यः परितस् तटद्रुमान्
प्रवृद्धवेगैः सलिलैर् अनिर्मलैः।
स्त्रियः सुदुष्टा इव जातविभ्रमाः
प्रयान्ति नद्यस् त्वरितम् पयोनिधिम्॥ २-७

'Flush with rain and monsoon mud, the rivers rush oceanwards with the earthy abandon of maidens chasing their lovers, every bit as heedless of their clucking kinsfolk as the torrents are of the trees they uproot as they race by.'

– Kalidasa, ritusamhara ('medley of the seasons'), fifth century CE

अद्यापि तां हरिणलोचनचञ्चलाक्षीं
मन्दारपुष्पचयशेखरचारुकेशीम् ।
उत्फुल्लनीलनलिनोदरकोमलाङ्गीं
संसारपाशमुदितो हि सतां स्मरामि ॥ २६ ॥

'Ah!, In those days when I might so, at rest,
Gaze in the eyes like roe's eyes, drink my fill
of her mouth's honey; from her jasmine breast
inhale the delicate fragrance, what they will
the Gods could do! I asked none of their bliss
Nor any heavenly feasting more than this.'

Bilhana, charaupanchasika ('love thief', tr. Edwin Arnold), eleventh century CE

अयमेकोऽहमेकेति ज्ञानं तत्संगमे न मे। राग
एवाधिकस्तत्र हृद्राचूर्णयोरिव॥

'The thought "I am one, she is one" disappears when love unites us.'

– *Anonymous*

समानप्रकृतिभावात् पुंसः स्त्रीणां च समं सुखम् ।
तस्मात् तां कामयेतैव यो हि तन्मन्यते तदा ॥

'Men and women, being of the same nature, feel the same kind of pleasure and therefore a man should marry such a woman as will love him ever afterwards.'

– Vatsayana, 'Kama Sutra' ('Principles of Love'), c. third century CE

कलर्हिःपं सुरतमचक्षते
वविादात्मकत्वाद्रामशीलत्वाच्च कामस्य।

'Sexual intercourse can be compared to a quarrel, on account of the contrarieties of love…'

– Vatsayana, Kama Sutra ('Principles of Love'), c. third century CE

न जातु कामः कामानामुपभोगेन शाम्यति ।
हविषा कृष्णवर्त्मेव भूय एवाभिवर्धते ॥ ९४ ॥

'Desire is never to be appeased by the enjoyment of that desire. Rather, it is fed just as the fire is by clarified butter.'

– *Manusmriti, c. second century CE*

यच्छे दाडमनसी प्राज्तस्तयज्टे जज्ञान आत्मनि ।
ज्ञानमात्मनि महति नियच्छे त्तधच्चे च्छान्त
आत्मनि ॥

'Let the wise subdue his speech by mind, subdue his mind by that nature which is knowledge; subdue his knowledge in the great soul, subdue this also in the placid soul.'

– Talavakara Upanishad, c. fifth century BCE

दादत्वं प्रयिवक्तृत्वं धीरत्वमुचतिज्ञता ।
श्रभ्यासेन न लभ्यते चत्वारस्सदजागुणाः ॥

'Liberality, sweetness of speech, courage, judgement:
these four natural qualities are not attained by practice.'

– *Anonymous*

न हि मुखं दुःखैर्विना लभ्यते ॥

'No pleasure is won without pain.'

– *Traditional*

ओदुंबराणा पुष्याणा शेतवणच्च वायसं ।
मव्यपादं जलें पश्येननारीहृद्वस्थतं ॥

'Life dribbles away like water from a leaky vessel.'

– *Bhartrihari, fifth century CE*

नीचो बदति न कुरुते न वदति कुरुते सज्जनः॥

'A mean fellow promises but does not.
A good man promises not but does.'

– *Anonymous*

परोपि हितवान् बंधुः ॥

'Though not of your kin, a friend is your truest relation.'

– Indian proverb

आत्मच्छिद्रं न जानंति परच्छिद्रानुसारिणः॥

ॐ

‘They know not their own defects
who look for defects in others.’

– *Indian proverb*

तावच्च शोभते मूर्खा यावत्किंचिन्न भाषते ॥

'A fool shines, so long as he says nothing.'

Indian proverb

उत्सादस्सादमं धयं वुद्वशि्शक्तां: पराक्रमः।
षडेते यच्च तषि्ठंतां तच्च देवोर्पां तषि्टतां॥

'Perseverance, daring, courage, wisdom, strength, and valour – where these six things are, there is God.'

– *Anonymous*

नमन्ति फलिनो वृक्षा नमन्ति गुणिनो जनाः ॥

'Nobody knows everything.'

– *Ancient Indian saying*

पुरूषकारमनुवर्तते दैवम् ।।

'Fortune follows human effort.'

प्राणमे व परित्यज्य मानमे वाभिरि चत् ु ।
अनित्यौ भवता प्राणो मान् रात्तद्रतारकं ॥

'Even at the cost of life, a man should preserve his honour.
Life is transient, honour as enduring as the moon and stars.'

– *Anonymous*

राजवत्पंचवर्षाणि दशवर्षाणि दासवत् ।
प्राप्ते तु षोडशे वर्षे पुत्रं मित्रवदाचरेत् ॥

A son should be treated as a prince for five years, as a slave for ten years and, in his sixteenth year, as a friend.

– Indian proverb

सर्वस्य गाचस्य शरिः प्रधानं ॥

'In the whole body, the head is chief.'

– *Indian proverb*

रजसा प्रफध्यते नारी काष्ठं ग्रएभ्यते तक्षणात् ।
ताम्रमस्तस्य योगेन पया वातेन एष्यते ॥

'Wood is rendered beautiful by chiselling;
copper corroded to a polish by tamarind;
the road cleaned by the scouring action of the wind.'

– Anonymous

यस्य नास्ति खयं प्रज्ञा णास्त्रं तस्य करोति किं ॥

'What will the wisest scripture do for him
who has no sense of his own?'

– *Anonymous*

बहूनपि गुणानेको दोषो ग्रसति ।।

'A single defect overshadows many qualities.'

– Chanakya, c. fourth century BCE

अवद्यायामन्तरे वत्तमानाः स्वयं धीराः
पण्डतित्तम्मन्यमानाः ।जद्घन्यमानाः परयिन्ति मूढा
अन्धेनैव नीयमाना यथान्धाः ॥

'In the midst of ignorance, fools, fancying themselves wise and learned, go round and round, oppressed by misery, as blind people led by a blind man.'

– Mundaka Upanishad, c. fifth century BCE

रथेन स्वै वशाः।

'All are made subject by money.'

– Indian proverb

श्‌रन्‌यारभः चे मकरः॥

‘A small beginning is good.’

– *Traditional saying*

आयुर्याति दिनं दिनं ॥

'Life goes day by day.'

– *Traditional saying*

कर्मणा बाध्यते बुद्धिर्न बुद्ध्या कर्म बाध्यते ॥

'The mind is ruled by fate, not fate by the mind.'

– *Anonymous*

उत्तरच जले पारे नौकया का प्रयोजनं ॥

ॐ

'Once the stream has been crossed, what use is the boat?'

– Indian proverb

उत्सादस्सारमं धेयं वुद्वशि्शक्ताः पराक्रमः ।
षडेते यत तष्ठिंता ततर देवोर्पा तष्ठिता ॥

'A plan considered by man in one way
is considered by God in another.'

– *Anonymous*

णव्रणकलंकानां काले लोपो भवव्ियता॥

'Debt, a sore, and a stain will be erased with time.'

– Indian proverb

दष्णावधि को गतः ॥

'Who ever reached the limit of his desire?'

– *Anonymous*

त्यजेदेकं कुलस्यार्थे ग्रामस्यार्थे कुलं त्यजेत्।
ग्रामं जनपदस्यार्थे आत्मार्थे पृथिवीं त्यजेत्॥

'You should forsake a man for the sake of your family; you should forsake your family for the sake of your village; you should forsake your village for the sake of your country; you should forsake the earth for the sake of yourself.'

– *Anonymous*

नास्तर्ा रामः क ुतस्सीमा नास्तर्ा वद्िया क ुतो चशः।
नात्तर्ा ज्ञानं क ुतो म ुक्तर्िभक्तर्िनास्तर्ा
क ुतस्त ु धोः!

'There is no village – how can there be a boundary?
There is no learning – how can there be fame?
There is no wisdom – how can there be salvation?
There is no faith – how can there be understanding?'

– *Anonymous*

न चापत्यवमस्स्नरी न च दैवात्परं बलं।
न च वद्यिासमो वंधुनाहंकारात्यरो रपिुः ॥॥

'No love can equal the parent's for their child; no power is greater than that of fate; no relation matters more than knowledge; no enemy is greater than self-conceit.'

– Anonymous

नति्यं सन्नहिती शत्यः ॥

'Death is always present.'

– Ancient saying

Picture Credits

Alamy: 15 (Dinodia Photos), 25 (Findlay), 62 (Hector Christiaen)

Cleveland Museum of Art: 27, 28

Dreamstime: 46 (Prsntg), 48 (Mrallen), 52 (Rifberlin), 87 (Pzaxe), 91 (Thefinalmiracle)

Getty Images: 5 (Heritage Images), 11 (Biblioteca Ambrosiana/DEA), 13 (Dibyangshu Sarkar/AFP), 22 (Heritage Images), 43 (Jitendra Singh), 88 (Sepia Times/Universal Images Group)

Los Angeles County Museum of Art: 18, 19, 44, 70, 77, 93

Metropolitan Museum of Art, New York: 7, 9, 12, 14, 16, 20, 23, 24, 30, 31, 32, 34, 37-41, 47, 49, 54-57, 59, 61, 65-67, 69, 71, 73, 74, 78-85, 89, 90, 92, 94, 95

Minneapolis Institute of Art: 26, 50, 64, 86

Rijksmuseum, Amsterdam: 63, 76

Walters Art Museum, Baltimore: 8, 10, 17, 21, 33, 35, 51, 58, 60, 68, 72, 75

Wellcome Collection: 45, 53

Yale Center for British Art: 29, 36, 42